The Art of Nature

Reflections on the Grand Design

Photography by Bruce W. Heinemann

Essays by Tim McNulty

BARNES
&NOBLE
BOOKS
NEW YORK

Contents

Reflections on Photographing the Art of Nature

It is a magical place in the North Cascades of Washington State that I return to every year. The glaciated mountains rise sharply, forming deep valleys alive with a rich tapestry of old growth forest, cascading waterfalls, and abundant wildlife. Fed by the glaciers towering above, two immensely beautiful but powerful rivers carve their way through the landscape to their final rendezvous with the sea. Clouds drifting inland off the Pacific often cloak the terrain in a steeping mist. Though I have been there many times before, it never seems to be the same when I return. The light is softer, the rivers run faster, leaves are falling instead of budding. Only its magnificence and the lure of capturing something new remains constant.

The photographs I have taken here portray a vision of the wild, the remote, the untouched. They do not reveal the time I had to wait for the dust of a passing car to settle, or show my quick sprint across the road to clear the path of a logging truck rumbling around the corner.

When I pause long enough to reflect upon my photographic inclinations, I realize that I rarely photograph subject matter that is more than a short walk or climb from my parked van. Indeed, as I look at my overall body of work, it seems ironic that the beauty that attracts me is so readily accessible.

My deep and abiding reverence for nature is exceeded only by my concern for its long-term viability and health. Perhaps for this reason, I choose to photograph in environments touched by the hand of man. I feel an urgency to explore those realms of nature most impacted by our presence. Indeed, I think it is critical for all of us to realize that we are not separate from nature, we are an intimate part of it.

The pursuit of photography is a richly rewarding and enlightening experience. It is not really about taking pictures per se. It is more of a journey, a search, for the greater realization of how our species is meant to relate to this "grand design."

It is clear that at this point in history, the family of man struggles with the issue of economic activity and environmental health. While the questions may be complex, the ultimate answer is quite simple: our species must engage in indefinitely sustainable economies to exist in harmony with the global ecosystem.

Creating sustainable economies is a process in which we must all participate. Perhaps the place to start is within each of us, taking a look at our planet anew and seeing our relationship to it and each other as inseparable. Perhaps this realization will guide us in our effort to create a civilization at peace with itself and in harmony with our home, Planet Earth.

Bruce W. Heinemann

Dedicated to my wife Judy and our newborn son

I'd walked the path hundreds of times in the years that I lived there, but one night continues to burn in my memory like a flame. Home then was a cabin in the woods by a small stream a mile's walk from the road. I might easily have walked the path blindfolded; I nearly had, more than one moonless night when I'd forgotten a flashlight or lamp. So the prospect of a walk on that clear, cold winter night, with the moon nearly full, was inviting.

It was early January. A chill arctic high had moved down from the north and settled over our usually rainy winter landscape like a lens of ice. Brush and dry grasses alongside the trail crackled with frost; the trail itself seemed to sparkle as it wound in and out of moonlight shadows. The sky was starry and deep, and the open, second growth forest took on a crystalline luster. I remember stopping to examine a frond of sword fern that had fallen over the trail; its patterned leaves were rimed with frost crystals as delicate as etched glass. Scattered leaves gathered moonlight from the forest floor, and the bare, frosted stems of salmonberry and willow seemed lit from within.

I don't remember how long I crouched there, but when I stood up, the sere and awesome beauty of the winter night took hold of me. Each alder along the trailside glowed with its own luminous pattern of pale silver and burnished white. Above them a thousand branches stretched a diamond net across the stars, while the branch tips of the fir trees burned with a lustrous blue light. The brilliance and clarity of the moon was overwhelming.

When I finally arrived at the clearing where my cabin sat among a few tall, frostlit trees, I was reluctant to go in in spite of the cold.

What is it that makes the familiar and day-to-day world become suddenly charged with beauty? And what process in each of us turns our vision away from that mystery to focus instead on the tasks at hand, purposeful, productive, and numb? I've considered these questions often in the years since my morning commute was a walk through the woods. And I know that those rare moments of vision were the times when the nature of this world, and my place within it, were most clear to me. But the question of nature's arresting beauty persists: What is its deeper meaning? And how does it, or rather, how do our deeply personal responses to nature, inform and guide our relationship with the natural world, both as individuals and as a society?

In his essay "Marshland Elegy," the visionary American conservationist Aldo Leopold mused on the meaning of beauty in nature. "Our ability to perceive quality in nature begins, as in art, with the pretty," he wrote. "It expands through successive stages of the beautiful to values as yet uncaptured by language." Leopold, as much a philosopher as a scientist, was looking for the deeper, ethical implications of that familiar stirring the natural world elicits in all of us at certain times. His writings strove to give voice to that vision, and his influence on the way Americans look at the natural world has been profound.

What do our hearts tell us in the flush of emotion we feel watching the dawn mist rise along a secluded lakeshore, or the footprint of moonlight step gingerly across the undulant waters of a quiet bay? We've all savored times like these; we've followed our feelings from contentment to peace, from a sense of empathy and wonder to those uncaptured values Leopold sought. Then, as now, such emotions are difficult to put into words. Yet if I trust anything, it is precisely those feelings: stirrings of recognition and oneness that well up from a source deeper than language. From these must come the values and ethics that guide our actions, if we and our earth will abide.

The wisdom of nature speaks to us heart to heart, and nature's first language is beauty. Complexity, richness, diversity...these also, to be sure, but they are articulations of the intellect. Beauty remains the language of the heart, and each of us perceives it in a slightly different way. For my part, I've employed a personal tutor in the art of seeing. What my young daughter lacks in years she makes up for in attention to the world at hand. In her eyes the world is perennially lit with frost and moonlight, and each fir cone or pebble of quartz, each meandering beetle or ant calls forth nothing less than rapt involvement. As I accompany her on her explorations, I'm learning once again to pay attention to what's at hand. And I'm finding the mysteries that lie at our feet can be as profound and involving as any grand or dramatic landscape; they just require a closer look.

A closer look at landscapes near at hand is nature photographer Bruce Heinemann's particular calling. The magic captured in his lens is heightened, for me, by the knowledge that he rarely has to travel very far to find it. Bruce's photographs depict a world neither remote nor inaccessible. Rather, his landscapes appear recognizable and easy to find. He offers visions of the world we might see in our daily travels, or a short weekend trip; a stunning world awaiting only our time and attention: alder trees in snow, hayfields in frost, wetlands, gardens, second growth woods. Places wild and undisturbed, and places showing ample evidence of human use. As important as the landscapes in Bruce's photographs are details: droplets on spider webs; frost patterns on a pane of glass; reeds in a vernal pond. He makes a point of frequently photographing close to a road, reexamining the familiar to find what might lie hidden there. As a result, his photographs refresh our perspective on the world "just past the doorstep," pointing gently toward what we might have missed.

Like a child's fascination, or the sudden awakening of moonlight on a frosty winter night, the artistry of nature continues to capture our imaginations. As it invites us to look again at the natural world, perhaps we will see how we might fit into its rhythms in a new, more appropriate way. That is the invitation nature, in all her grace and beauty, holds out to us now. It's an offering, without strings attached, but the way in which we choose to respond will in no small way determine our future—and hers.

As I crouched among the frost-sheathed ferns, and felt the presence of the winter night enter my blood, I remember thinking that we are, in all our rushed insistence, still new to the country of earth. Our species emerged in a time of ice and darkness, and the tracks of our passage haven't yet melted from the snow. Perhaps it's time we stopped, midstride amidst the noise and clutter of our time, and let the coolness of the morning embrace us. If we only take the time to look closely at the beauty of this nurturing world, look with the eyes we were born with, we can't help but recognize it as home.

14

The Gift of Rain

The rain let up just before dawn and a low mist hung among the reeds and winter brush. We followed a tractor road in the early darkness, and watched as the dawn broke over a wide marshland and estuary where a small stream entered a saltwater bay. At first we couldn't see them, but soon the early light revealed a field cobbled with the huddled shapes of thousands of migratory ducks.

My friend, a biologist who manages this small reserve, identified several species from their quiet murmurings as they began to feed: mallard, green-winged teal, pintail. Farther off, on the open water, were widgeon and merganser. Most were stopping here to feed and rest on their winter journey south, but many would stay.

As we moved closer, the small band of ducks nearest us burst upward in a whir of wing beats. Another band followed, then another—like a chain of explosions—until the sky was thick with rising birds wheeling back and forth over the marsh, and the morning silence shattered with the thunder of their wings. The birds moved in billows and waves across the field and marsh until, just as suddenly, they coasted back down, settled, and quietly continued to feed.

A light rain began to move back in, and the cloud cover lowered over the marsh like a protective quilt.

The importance of wetlands as habitats for migratory and nesting birds was recognized in the early years of this century when Theodore Roosevelt set aside some of our country's first wildlife sanctuaries. Only later, with the development of the science of ecology, came a deeper understanding of the relationship between these areas and the larger ecosystems of which they're a part. Productive coastal estuaries like this one were found to be linked to farmlands, residential areas, and cities, as well as forested headwaters. They're as dependent upon sound forestry and farming practices as they are upon good wildlife management. Ecologically, these varied elements are joined together in a single functioning system called a watershed.

A watershed is an area of land where all the rain or snow that falls drains to a common outlet—a river, lake, or bay. Watersheds are the terrestrial link in the hydrologic cycle, the complex exchange of moisture between ocean, atmosphere, and land. It's a system as old as the earth. Molecules of water were among the original compounds of the solar system. The oceans, products of earth's

atmosphere, are nearly as old. Two to three billion years ago, there was as much water on earth as there is today. More to the point, it's the same water.

The finely balanced maintenance systems of the biosphere are elegant in their workings, and the hydrologic cycle is no exception. Simply put, the hot, tropical sun of the equatorial regions evaporates tremendous amounts of water from the oceans. The same thermal transfer also gives birth to winds and ocean currents. In that lower part of the earth's atmosphere called the troposphere, this heat-driven weather system transfers enormous amounts of energy from tropic to polar regions, moderating the earth's temperature and climate.

As warm, moisture-laden air from the oceans rises against coastal and inland ranges of the continents, it cools, releasing its burden of rain and snow, feeding rivers, lakes, groundwater, and streams—renewing and replenishing watersheds.

At any time, less than one percent of the earth's moisture is available as fresh, flowing water; the rest remains in salt seas or locked in arctic icecaps. Yet this small amount, filtering through the leaves and rootlets of countless watersheds, is what makes the rich mosaic of life on earth possible. No matter where we live, we're part of a watershed, and any human activity on any part of a watershed has the potential to affect the whole.

I've come to think of watersheds as living things, bodies through which the timeless dance of the seas, clouds, and weather reveals itself. Yet this cycle of water, this gift the rain brings, is so common to our existence it has almost become invisible, so common that, in many parts of the world, its very health is threatened.

Though we've protected some important wetlands as habitat in this country, we've lost more than half our wetlands to agriculture and residential and urban development. The invaluable functions these wetlands performed, such as floodwater retention, water purification, groundwater recharge, and streamflow maintenance, not to mention fish and wildlife habitat, were also lost.

We know better now, but unless this knowledge translates into a shared sense of common stewardship, it will prove of little use. It's only when we take this kind of knowledge into our hearts, those parts of us already touched by the beauty of the natural world, that we begin to see with the uncommon clarity necessary to protect these natural gifts and pass them along unspoiled.

The ecological lessons we are learning now are not new lessons. Nearly four thousand years ago the people of China learned, tragically, that when uplands were stripped of forest cover, river valleys and the farming villages that grew up around them became much more subject to floods, soil erosion, and drought. In the centuries that followed, the same pattern was repeated in Mesopotamia, Crete, Greece, Cyprus, Rome, and the Mediterranean basin, as well as in England and the New World.

As recently as a decade ago in the Pacific Northwest, riparian areas—the lush vegetative zones that border rivers, lakes, and streams—were shorn of the large trees needed for stream stabilization and fish and wildlife habitat. Riparian vegetation, which covers less than one percent of western North America, provides habitats for more bird species than all other vegetation types combined. Like wetlands, riparian areas were cleared for agriculture, road development, and town sites. Their benefits, too, were poorly understood. Now, with the sharp decline of salmon stocks in the Northwest, and the specter of drought troubling much of the western United States, the benefits of stable stream corridors and upland forests are understood very well.

As our numbers continue to increase and available resources dwindle, we are beginning to realize the cost of rapid growth and our high standard of living. We see it in the decline in the quality of our water and air, in the loss of forests, fish, and wildlife, and in the chemicals in our soils and groundwater.

It's true that, as a society, we've taken some important first steps toward protecting the natural systems that sustain us. But it's also true that we've been slow to learn the more subtle and elemental lesson of how to live with the earth, consciously as watershed residents, and responsibly as members of a larger natural community. We've yet to curb our propensities toward consumption and convenience, and replace them with a commitment to live in a sustainable manner, to conserve, recycle, reuse. These kinds of cultural transformations don't lend themselves to a legislative fix. Rather, they must become part of who we are, individually and as a people.

The earth and sky offer freely their gift of rain. Like so many of the earth's gifts—the magic of sunlight, the fertility of the land, the great blessing of life itself—it must be held, cared for, and ultimately given away. For only by passing the gift along can the great cycles continue. And only in letting go are the deepest lessons of life learned.

As the rain deepened over the marsh and the ducks continued to feed, my friend told me that it's only for a week or two each year that this many migratory birds visit the marsh. Much of the rest of his time is spent growing grain or otherwise managing the area for this winter visitation. But being able to start his day by coming out and seeing them wake as the morning breaks is all the reward he needs.

As we turned and started back up the tractor road, I thought that these brief glimpses of nature's beauty are also gifts of a kind, blessings from a world outside ourselves to the world within. Of course, it's one singular world in nature's grand design, and the gift of beauty, like the gift of rain, will continue to return as long as we've eyes to see it.

44

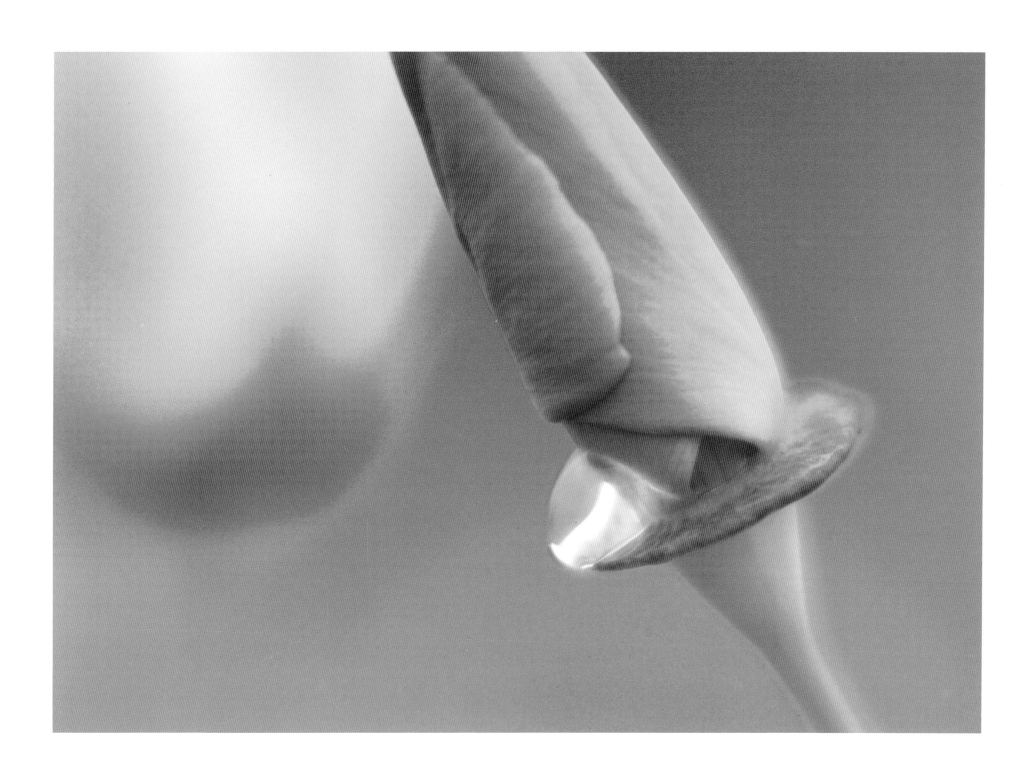

74

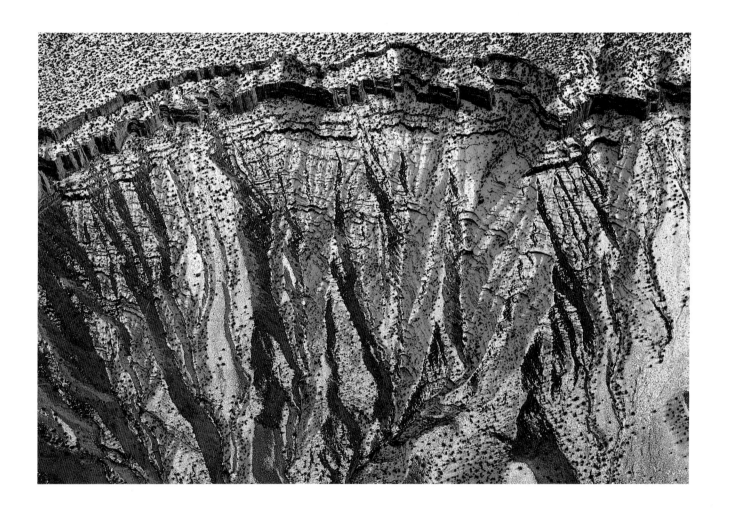

The Wind's Question

In those corners of the world where rainfall is plentiful, nature's green abundance crowds the landscape shoulder to shoulder. Forest, field, and farmland bear leafy witness to the bounty brought by rain. Mountain ranges strain the clouds of their rain and snow, but rainfall tapers dramatically on the leeward slopes. Forests of juniper and pine give way to bunch grass and sage. Such arid regions cover vast inland areas, including most of the intermountain West.

Dry landscapes tend to be less curvaceous and lush; the bones of the earth show through. The beauty of arid country speaks more of light and distance; of open spaces pruned and polished by the wind. It's a subtler beauty, one that rises slowly to the eye: softened tones of redrock and sage; fluidity of dunes and canyon walls; snow, rock, and sparse desert trees. Yet the beauty of these lands also speaks on a deeper level. Its scarps and folds and river-cut canyons reveal traces of the geologic origins of the land. The procession of ancestral rivers and seas, lava plains, and desert sands is incised into the bedrock of these lands like the lines of a shell.

It was the spare glacial landscapes of the Pleistocene that drew the first of our kind to this continent. Not surprisingly, the early signs of our passage, and the cultural adaptations by which we learned to live here, have been best preserved in arid lands. They serve as a reminder that we too are passing through. When considering the path by which we've come, and the crowded plain that lies ahead, my thoughts frequently turn to the desert.

It wasn't long ago, amid the austere beauty of a desert canyon, that I had a fleeting glimpse of the passage of a culture through a landscape. From a ledge high on a canyon wall, I looked out over a low delta where a side canyon entered the Colorado River. The delta sloped gently toward the muddy flow of the river, and a band of small trees traced the water's edge. An evening shadow moved across the canyon floor but the river caught a burnt-copper light reflecting from the rimrock and shimmered with an iridescence all its own. The canyon walls rose silently around me toward a pale and distant sky.

In spring, when snow melts from the canyon rim, this small side canyon swells briefly with runoff. It was then that the people who once lived here were able to cultivate this delta, diverting water through a series of check dams and canals, and bring the narrow canyon floor into bloom. Fields of corn, beans, and squash were meticulously tended, watered by hand from the river as summer progressed. Crops did well in the heat of the canyon, and the people thrived.

Behind me, tucked into the base of a redwall cliff, five small windowlike openings marked the remnants of the village's granary. Once filled with clay pots sealed against shortage or drought, the granary now stood empty and open to the wind. A shift in rainfall patterns and an extended drought some 800 years ago forced the people to leave this canyon in search of more dependable water sources. A few broken piles of rock, shards of pottery, a *metate* or grinding stone, are all that remains of their village site. Those, and the ever-present ravens calling back and forth across the canyon shadows.

The movement of people and cultures across the North American continent has been as fluid and shifting as the land itself. Not far from the village site, in the canyon's depths, are rock strata that date back nearly half the age of the earth. Once folded and uplifted into a vast range of mountains, they were weathered by water, ice, and wind to a sea-level plain. Over the next two billion years, the plain was inundated by seas and coastlines, river deltas and desert dunes, fault-block ranges and volcanic cones. Each of these landscapes in turn was worn and weathered smooth by the slow but relentless forces of time. The eternal rhythms of deposition and erosion are incised into these canyon walls like a musical score.

These striate walls also tell another story. A record of the evolution of life on this planet was written into the sedimentary strata, from simple algae in the early marine limestones, to reptiles and amphibians in the upper sandstones. It's a wondrous story—of diversity, adaptation, and change—and it holds truths as poignant to us in this century as to those who passed this way centuries before.

It's hard to imagine a people living out their existence amid the spare and timeless beauty of the arid canyon country of the West without being profoundly touched by it, just as we are today. The beauty those farming people found in their canyon home is reflected in the rock art that still adorns the canyon walls, and in their intricately patterned pottery, considered today to be among the most exquisite in North America. But there were earlier artifacts, left by a culture that preceded theirs, that

also bear eloquent witness to the beauty that shapes a people's existence.

Nearly four thousand years ago, the canyon country was home to small nomadic groups of hunting people. Theirs wasn't an easy existence; their tools were rudimentary and game was often scarce. But in high caves among the canyon walls, they left talismans of their hunting magic: small, split-twig figurines, woven from a single cotton-wood or willow twig, often in the shape of a desert bighorn sheep, deer, or antelope. Some had pellets of deer scat in them; others were pierced with twigs resembling spears. Thus did these early wayfarers record their reverence for the mystery, power, and grace of the life forms on which they depended. Like clay pots of grain sealed into canyon walls, the

figurines were these people's prayer for survival, magic being the only currency they had.

Our passage here—from small migratory groups in pursuit of game, to a large urban society, migratory in a different kind of way, and in pursuit of something less readily defined—has occurred in a flash of geologic time. The human record is a thin glaze on the earth's crust, a patina depicting a species struggling to fit and passing the knowledge along.

Like the cultures that preceded us on this continent, we tend to our needs and try, in good times, to put a little something by. In place of talismans, we've fashioned institutions to shore our fortunes against an uncertain future, and we've been successful. There are more of us now, enjoying a

81

higher standard of living (by world standards) than ever before. But, looking out across the canyon that evening, a nagging question persisted: *For how long?* The old cultures flourished because they were sustainable—implicitly in touch with the climate, resource base, and needs of their population. Our current way of life, with its reliance on limited fossil fuels, chemically subsidized agriculture, and an ever-increasing thirst for world resources, begs the question; how long can it be sustained?

There's little doubt that our society must ultimately reconcile itself with the limits of the natural systems that surround us. This much is crucial. There's less agreement over how that can be done. On the most basic level, it can only come about when each of us becomes intently aware of

the richness, fragility, and presence of the natural world. It's something each culture must discover anew, in its own distinctive way, and, like the cultures that went before us, we have as our teacher the unerring beauty of nature to guide us.

It's believed that the people who left the canyon 800 years ago settled in the mesa country to the east to become the ancestors of the Hopi people. The Hopi still live among the beautiful mesas, tending their crops and carrying on their centuries-old religious traditions. Their village of Oraibi, founded around 1200 A.D. is the oldest continually occupied settlement in North America. Theirs is a culture steeped and grounded in place like few others in North America. If there is a model for sustainability, it might lie hidden in

their cultural wisdom, in their gentle reverence for earth and sky.

As the evening shadow lengthened, a cool wind moved down the side canyon, skirting my ledge, and rustling the dry grasses at my feet. I listened as it fluted through the empty granary behind me with a low, lilting sound, stirring a little dust in its wake. It was as if the wind that fell from the high canyon rim, that caressed and polished all the ageless strata of the canyon walls, to reach me, were asking, "What have you set aside for the future? How will your people live with this land?"

A wisp of sand brushed my knee before it vanished in the depths of the canyon. And the river rolled past beneath me, quiet as the stars.

91

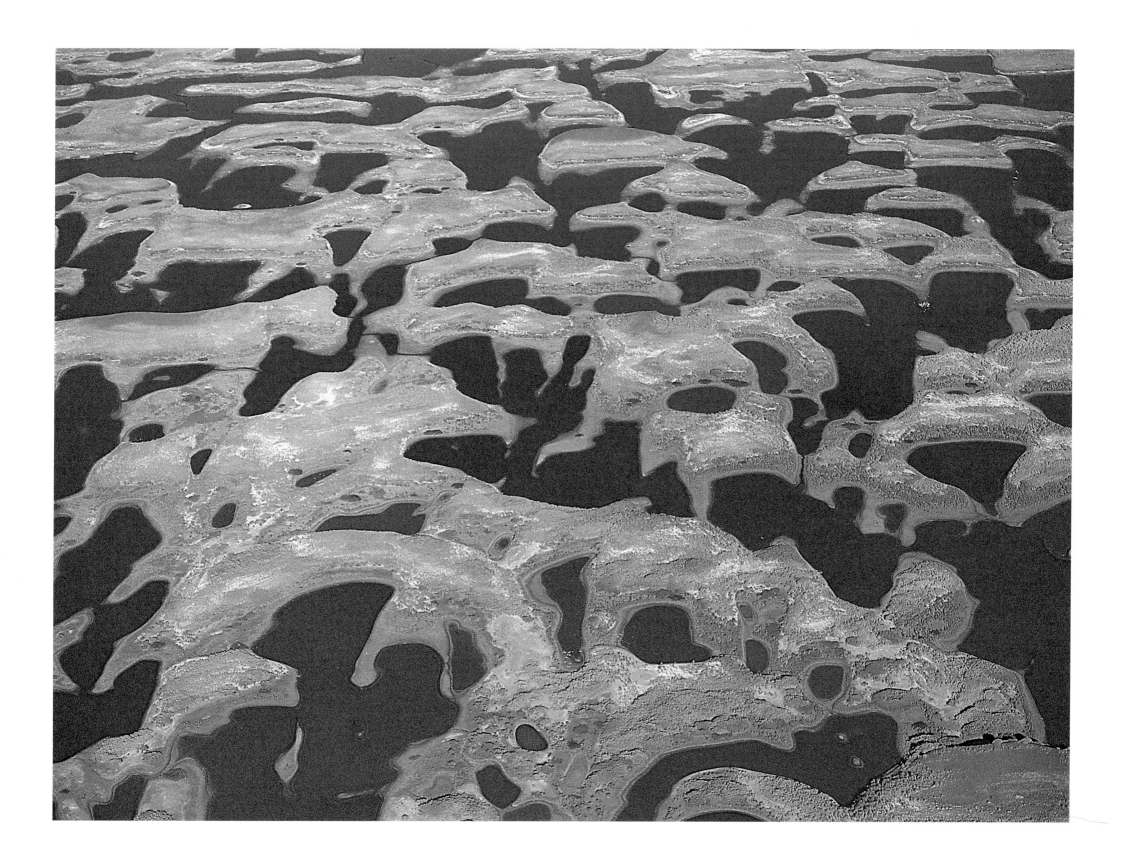

Occasionally I like to pull out images of one location I have photographed over a period of time. Reviewing them together often reveals things about my photographic experience of which I might not be fully aware. The actual time I spend shooting is regrettably little, about three days a month. Consequently from my "menu" of potential photographic locations, I tend to choose familiar places that offer a great deal of visual variety. The results of this pattern form a body of work that depicts much of the character and ecology of my oft-visited locations.

I create slideshows for my multimedia concerts, and seeing groups of images rather than smaller selections from edits, seems to produce a larger, more expansive perspective of the natural world. I find this process of review and feedback helpful in obtaining an overall view of how my photography is progressing. It also perhaps bears witness to my changing perception of and relationship to nature.

When I look at my most recent images at any given point in time, the question always arises: what is the quality of these images that render them personally more satisfying? Is it the light, the composition, the subjects I choose? Perhaps it is better technique. Maybe I see more deeply than before, or, maybe I'm just getting luckier? Part of the answer may lie in these possibilities. However, I think the greater truth resides in something more fundamental. This issue always leads me back to the essence of my work and begs the larger question, why do I photograph? It is not easily answered in words, but I can say that my photography is a study of relationships. It is an ongoing lesson taught by nature about the wonderfully complex web of life of which we are a part. I believe it is natural that this learning process manifests itself in the photographic image.

In teaching photography to the eager student, it is the greatest challenge to help them shift their focus from mostly technical considerations to the deeper and more essential aspects of this art. It is often difficult to convince the student that the "why do I take this picture" is more important than the "how do I take this picture."

The images in the book were mostly taken in the past year with a few from as far back as five years. My challenge for this project was to try to go beyond the limitations of my experience and open myself up to seeing the natural world from a larger and more mature perspective. As with any creative endeavor there were many moments of joy and satisfaction as well as times of frustration and setbacks. Overall I am happy with this collection of work. I hope that you will find these images enjoyable and informative.

I prefer to work with the absolute minimum amount of equipment necessary. The images here are a mix of 35mm, 6 x 7, and 4 x 5 formats. I used a Nikon FE2 body with 24mm, 55mm macro, and 80-200mm zoom, and 300mm lenses and extension tubes. In medium format I used a Pentax 67 body and Pentax 45mm, 135mm macro, and 200mm lenses. In large format I used a Linhof Techna field camera with 137mm and 210mm Scheider lenses. Early in the book project, I discontinued the use of large format in favor of medium format to compliment my 35mm gear. I found 4 x 5 to be cumbersome and not well suited to the telephoto work I like to do. Near the completion of this book

all of my gear was stolen. I subsequently elected to downsize my equipment further by combining all of my focal lengths into two new lenses, a 24-50mm zoom and a 75-300mm zoom, both Nikkors. I replaced my Pentax 67 system intact.

Until several years ago I used Kodachrome 25. Feeling that I was missing many shots in low or unusual light, I gave up the fine grain of K25 for the even tones and color saturation of Fuji 50. I got excellent results with this film and used it until Fuji came out with its new Velvia. This film has turned out to be the finest yet and I now use it exclusively.

Plates

With Gratitude

I would like to express my sincerest appreciation to Ted Mader and Associates

for their unending support and participation in The Art of Nature project.

Also a special thank you to Scott Hudson for his dedicated effort to this book.

To Tim McNulty: my deepest appreciation for your gift of vision, sensitivity,

and eloquence.

— *B R U C E   H E I N E M A N N*

P R I O R   P U B L I S H I N G

The Art of Nature: Reflections on the Grand Design

This edition published by Barnes & Noble, Inc.,
by arrangement with Prior Publishing

1998 Barnes & Noble Books

ISBN 0-07607-1031-7

M10987654321

Direct all inquiries to Bruce Heinemann at Prior Publishing

Published by
Prior Publishing
16010 197th Ave. N.E.
Woodinville, WA 98072
(800)786-6359

All photographs and text of Reflections on Photographing the Art of Nature
© 1992 Bruce W. Heinemann

Essays © 1992 TIm McNulty

Design by Ted Mader + Associates

Printed in Hong Kong through Palace Press, San Francisco, CA.